DEDICATION

To Gordon and Bea Schulenburg and Jeff and Pam Burkett. When I think of you...I believe God has blessed Cyndi and me with wonderful parents, and I thank him for the wisdom and love you've shown to us throughout the years. I'm blessed in so many ways because of you, and I'm grateful for the years I've had with you. I love you.

When I...

500 Sentence-Finishers
to Get Your
Students Talking

Brian Schulenburg

ZONDERVAN®

ZONDERVAN.com/
AUTHORTRACKER
follow your favorite authors

youth
specialties

**youth
specialties**

When I...: 500 Sentence-Finishers to Get Your Students Talking
Copyright 2009 by Youth Specialties

Youth Specialties resources, 300 S. Pierce St., El Cajon, CA 92020 are published by
Zondervan, 5300 Patterson Ave. SE, Grand Rapids, MI 49530.

Library of Congress Cataloging-in-Publication Data

Schulenburg, Brian.
  When I— : 500 sentence-finishers to get your students talking / Brian
Schulenburg.
      p. cm.
  ISBN 978-0-310-28327-0 (pbk.)
  1. Discussion in Christian education. 2. Christian education of young
people. 3. Church group work with youth. I. Title.
  BV1534.5.S38 2008
  268'.433—dc22

                                                                    2008028004

Web site addresses listed in this book were current at the time of publication. Please
contact Youth Specialties via email (YS@YouthSpecialties.com) to report URLs that are
no longer operational and provide replacement URLs if available.

Cover design and interior design by SharpSeven Design

Printed in the United States of America

---

09 10 11 12 13 14 • 20 19 18 17 16 15 14 13 12 11 10 9 8 7 6 5 4 3 2 1

PREFACE

I don't know about you, but I love youth ministry. As a student ministries pastor for more than 15 years now, I've worked with thousands of students. During that time, I've learned that the most effective moments I spend with students happen when I get them in a small group and ask them questions.

Have you ever wondered what your students would do if they were faced with certain choices? I love hearing about the things they're passionate about. I love listening to them describe how they handle life's challenges. I love listening to them talk about their dreams. And I could literally listen to students talk about their views on the world for hours. That's why I wrote this book—to help youth workers get into the hearts of their students.

I hope you'll enjoy asking these questions as much as I've enjoyed writing them. And hearing your students' responses to these questions will open your eyes, as you realize just how much you don't know about your students.

May God bless you on your journey through the world of student ministry!

In Him,

Brian Schulenburg

ACKNOWLEDGEMENTS

When I started writing books full of questions (during a van ride from Minneapolis to Chicago to spend Thanksgiving with my family), I never dreamed I'd be writing a third book for the Quick Questions series.

Over the years the questions in this book have been written in vans, buses, restaurants, my office, and my home. They've also been written in Guatemala, El Salvador, Honduras, Minnesota, Wisconsin, and Illinois. And many of the questions have been written because of someone else's contribution. So I want to say thank you to all of my students, friends, and family who've been a part of this journey.

I must also thank Jesus Christ, whose love compels me to share him with others. The fact that you died so we could be redeemed just blows me away. You are my Savior, my Friend, my Hero, and my Inspiration. Thank you for reaching out to me when I did nothing to deserve you.

Thanks, also, to Jay Howver and the team at Youth Specialties who've continued to put their faith in this author. You're a blessing in my life and in the lives of countless youth workers around the world.

Finally, thank you to the following people who all contributed at least one question to this book: Cyndi Schulenburg, Breanna Schulenburg, Christopher Schulenburg, Jeremy Schulenburg, Zachary Schulenburg, Greg Krech, Rick Krech, and Kayla Schaeffer. You helped me more than you'll ever know.

HOW TO USE *WHEN I...*

When I... is a finish-the-sentence book that's designed to be used as a discussion starter tool. Only you can determine how best to use it in your local context, but I've provided a few suggestions to get you started.

Pick a Number, Any Number

When using the books in the Quick Questions series, many youth workers will ask their students to pick a number between 1 and 500. Students love the random nature of the questions they receive. But make sure you read the question to yourself before reading it out loud to the group. Some questions may not be appropriate for all students.

Choose the Questions Ahead of Time

Some questions may fit a particular teaching theme or topic. Read through the questions and find ones that will tie in with an upcoming teaching series. Or you may think of certain students as you read through the questions. Pencil their initials next to the question and plan to ask it during your next event.

Road Trip, Anyone?

End those road trip arguments over the radio station once and for all. Bring along this book and let the conversation roll. It's amazing how much faster your road trip will go when you get students talking. And for some real fun, bring along the other books in Youth Specialties' Quick Questions series so you can pull questions from two or three books.

Campfire

No retreat is complete without a campfire. While you'll typically spend the end of the retreat talking about what God did over the course of your time together, gathering to answer some questions around the campfire could be an effective way to not only use this book, but also kick off your retreat. You'll gain invaluable knowledge about your students and get a jump-start on your weekend of group bonding.

In the Classroom

This book can also be used in church and school classrooms. Use it as part of your announcement time. Students will look forward to coming to class because they'll be able to find out more about each other, as well as the day's topic.

Small Groups

Like most youth workers, I have small-group leaders who feel comfortable leading conversations and others who dread it. This book is a great tool for either type of leader. Give copies to your small-group leaders and suggest that they use a couple of these discussion starters before they begin asking their regular list of questions. In no time at all, their group will be ready to roll!

Use Common Sense

Just a note of caution: I have several students who've never met their biological father. Therefore, it would be entirely inappropriate and insensitive for me to ask one of them to answer question number four: "When I spend time with my dad...." In a situation like this, you might consider rephrasing the question so it's asking about another male influence in their lives instead: "When I spend time with my small-group leader...."

I'd love to hear how you're using *When I...* in your own ministry setting. Feel free to send me an email at brian_schulenburg@yahoo.com and let me know how things are going.

God bless you, and happy Q & A!

1.   When I think about God...

2.   When I get to college, I'm most excited about...

3.   When I go on vacation...

4. When I spend time with my dad...

5. When I think about global warming...

6. When I purchase my next cell phone...

7. When I go to my youth group...

8.   When I surf the Internet...

9.   When I think about my biggest weakness...

10.   When I have a choice of flying, taking a train, or going by bus...

11.   When I play video games...

When I...

12. When I think about my future...

13. When I'm the boss...

14. When I think about my parents looking at my Facebook or MySpace account...

15. When I go to church...

16. When I get a chance to ask Jesus a question...

17. When I read the newspaper...

18. When I think about whom I'd most like to impress...

19. When I watch TV...

20. When I go for a walk...

21. When I feel afraid...

22. When I think about the last time I cried...

23. When I was a little kid and celebrated Valentine's Day at school...

24. When I hear politicians debate...

25. When I think about one thing I'd change about myself...

26. When I sin...

27. When I feel sick...

28.   When I get to heaven...

29.   When I sing karaoke...

30.   When I fight with my parents...

31.   When I think about the ultimate high school job...

32.   When I lose...

33.   When I grow up...

34.   When I feel like I don't fit in...

35.   When I think about the resurrection...

36.   When I'm at a party...

37.   When I watch the Super Bowl, I like...

38.   When I'm on a church retreat...

39.   When I Google my name...

40. When I see a friend who's hurting...

41. When I get a text message...

42. When I check my MySpace or Facebook account...

43. When I journal...

44. When I think about my senior year in high school...

45. When I read the Bible...

46. When I get straight As...

47. When I drive through a blizzard...

48. When I think about hell...

49. When I have a major paper due...

50. When I think about how I spend my money...

51. When I can't find something, it's usually...

52. When I play Monopoly, I'm the...

53. When I celebrate New Year's Eve, I usually...

54. When I think about college...

55. When I ask someone on a date for the first time...

56. When I get hurt, the first person I want to talk to is...

57. When I think about the Holy Spirit, I have questions about...

58. When I'm depressed...

59. When I see someone picking his or her nose...

When I...

60. When I believe my best friend is about to make the biggest mistake ever...

61. When I feel awkward...

62. When I meet someone new...

63. When I think about the Holocaust...

64. When I want to know the right thing to do...

65. When I don't know what to do...

66. When I think about Satan...

67. When I hear gossip...

68. When I play baseball...

69. When I think about the government...

70. When I was a baby...

71. When I'm at a school dance...

72. When I think about the thing I most like about myself...

73. When I go to McDonalds, I always order...

74. When I feel lonely...

75. When someone I know has died...

76. When I'm treated unfairly...

77. When I think about the biggest issues facing our country...

78. When I think about the biggest issues facing our world...

79. When I get goofy...

80. When I make supper...

81. When I hang out with my mom...

82. When I think about the 1980s...

83. When I get in a fight...

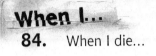

84. When I die...

85. When I walk into a crowded room...

86. When I can't find a parking space...

87. When I sing in the shower...

88. When I talk to my pastor...

89. When I go on a mission trip...

90. When I have a weird dream...

91. When I think about the next year of my life...

92. When I need guidance...

93. When I go to Starbucks, I order...

94. When I'm mad...

95. When I feel the closest to God is...

96. When I think about which infomercial product I might actually want to buy someday...

97. When I'm in a group, I see myself as a(n)...

98. When I think about my personality, I am...

99. When I visit a new school, the first thing I notice is...

100. When I graduate(d) from high school...

101. When I'm around people who don't look or act like I do...

102. When I think about my neighbors...

103. When I hear about endangered animals...

104. When I think about what my parents think about me...

105. When I go to a musical...

106. When I don't want to go to school...

107. When I feel most alive...

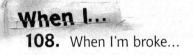

When I...

108. When I'm broke...

109. When I think about what I might become famous for...

110. When I get behind in a project...

111. When I see people who are on strike...

112. When I fall in love...

113. When I turn on the radio...

114. When I find out that my family has to move...

115. When I cry...

116. When I get a flat tire...

117. When I see someone from my past...

118. When I hear about drunk drivers...

119. When I think about pressure...

120. When I'm bored...

121. When I don't have access to the Internet...

122. When I see a clown...

123. When I'm with my friends...

124. When I see an elderly couple holding hands...

125. When I sleep...

126. When I quote Scripture...

127. When I volunteer...

128. When I have to confront someone...

129. When I vote for president...

130. When I have a craving for junk food...

131. When I go to the doctor's office, I hate...

132. When I'm standing in line...

133. When I think about my dream car...

134. When I pray for my family...

135. When I'm watching a scary movie...

136. When I ride my bike...

137. When I have to speak in front of a group...

138. When I'm tempted...

139. When I think about the worst gift I've ever received...

140. When I spend time with my grandparents...

141. When I lose my temper...

142. When I win...

143. When I hear somebody trash-talking...

144. When I'm at home...

145. When I hear the word *communism*...

146. When I get embarrassed...

147. When I feel God's love...

148. When I'm with a friend who does something I don't agree with...

149. When I wish upon a star...

150. When I feel the most secure...

151. When I'm in the snow...

152. When I see injustice...

153. When I think about modern-day slavery...

154. When I hear the word *theology*...

155. When I eat Thanksgiving dinner, I always...

156. When I receive a compliment...

157. When I'm at home with my siblings but without our parents...

158. When I think about the qualities I'm looking for in the person I'll marry...

159. When I stay up all night...

160. When I drink caffeine...

161. When I'm forced to dance...

162. When I see a beautiful person...

163. When I see a homeless person...

164. When I have to ask someone to do something for me...

165. When I see my favorite team losing...

166. When I go to a school sporting event...

167. When I see my parents kiss...

168. When I think about my favorite Christmas memories...

169. When I disagree with an authority figure...

170. When I think about moving out on my own...

171. When I'm around my relatives...

172. When I tell jokes...

173. When I think about my greatest strength...

174. When I baby-sit...

175. When I look at the stars...

176. When I work hard...

177. When I ride in the car while my dad's driving...

178. When I think about going to see a movie in the theater by myself...

179. When I have to spend time with people I don't like...

When I...

180. When I go on a road trip...

181. When I hear my parents fighting...

182. When I travel to a foreign country...

183. When I don't care...

184. When I have a piece of birthday cake...

185. When I'm 50 years old...

186. When I go out to eat...

187. When I think about the most extreme thing I've ever done...

When I...

188. When I'm at a lake...

189. When I'm with my best friends...

190. When I see someone smoking...

191. When I think about my wedding day...

192. When I watch a sunset...

193. When I see someone getting picked on...

194. When I think back to my first day at school...

195. When I think about my heroes...

196. When I get ready for church...

197. When I think about what it means to be a part of the body of Christ...

198. When I decorate the Christmas tree...

199. When I'm running late...

200. When I'm the underdog...

201. When I make art...

202. When I eat the school's lunch...

203. When I think about abortion...

204. When I'm confused...

205. When I have a math test...

206. When I tell my future children what time their curfew will be...

207. When I know I've disappointed my parents...

208. When I hear songs from *The Sound of Music*...

209. When I think about war...

210. When I see a car along the side of the road...

211. When I'm in an unfamiliar place...

212. When I'm near someone who's throwing up...

213. When I hear a choir singing...

214. When I confess my sins...

215. When I slip and fall on the ice...

216. When I have to use the restroom and all of the stalls are full...

217. When I'm around people drinking alcohol...

218. When I think about visionary leaders...

219. When I fly in an airplane...

220. When I go shopping for shoes...

221. When I see a mouse...

222. When I hear or read celebrity gossip...

223. When someone is tailgating me...

224. When I play Scrabble...

225. When I compare myself to others...

226. When I meditate upon a passage of Scripture...

227. When I get jealous...

228. When someone is mad at me...

229. When I'm asked to describe what's special about me...

230. When I drive...

231. When I watch an episode of *American Idol*...

232. When I'm around dogs...

233. When I hear about other religions...

234. When I'm punished...

235. When I impersonate someone, I like to pretend to be...

236. When I see famous celebrities destroying their lives...

237. When I pray...

238. When I hang around little kids...

239. When I feel like I'm not good enough...

240. When I go to a funeral...

241. When I hope...

242. When I eat Life Savers...

243. When I recycle...

244. When I get a friend request on MySpace or Facebook...

245. When I get dressed up for a formal...

246. When I see someone eating lunch alone...

247. When I read a history textbook...

248. When I eat spaghetti...

249. When I feel like my parents don't understand me...

250. When I decorate my room...

251. When I shop at iTunes...

252. When I think about the best prank I've ever heard of...

253. When I go to a youth conference...

254. When I get on a skateboard...

255. When I receive a paycheck the size of my dad's or my mom's paycheck...

256. When I think about my future family...

257. When I hear country music...

258. When I feel like giving up...

259. When I think about running a marathon...

260. When I watch a James Bond movie...

261. When I go fishing...

262. When I see a picture of myself...

263. When I get home after being gone for a while...

264. When I'm at school...

265. When I get sunburned...

266. When I receive junk email messages...

267. When I think about skydiving...

268. When I hear that a friend of mine is depressed...

269. When I listen to good music...

270. When I relax...

271. When I listen to a sermon...

272. When I think about what I collect...

273. When I first walked into my school's cafeteria...

274. When I listen to my parents complain about the high cell phone bill...

275. When I'm on a farm...

276. When I hear people at my school talk about Christians...

277. When I think about being a truck driver...

278. When I read, I go...

279. When I think about being in a small group Bible study...

280. When I watch cartoons...

281. When I go to a friend's church...

282. When I mistakenly say "Hi!" to someone, thinking that person is really someone else...

283. When I'm in the ocean...

284. When I want to have a great time with friends, I call...

285. When I feel like I've been lied about...

286. When I think about what the world will look like in 50 years...

287. When I see a child throwing a temper tantrum...

288. When I think about the second coming of Christ...

289. When I retire...

290. When I wake up in the morning...

291. When I think about the things that I do that make God happy...

292. When a nurse gives me a shot...

293. When I'm at an amusement park...

294. When I have to deal with changes in my life...

295. When I get pulled over for speeding...

296. When I see a butterfly...

297. When I think about counseling...

298. When I hear that someone I know has an eating disorder...

299. When I read about King David, a man after God's own heart, and his sins...

When I...

300. When I think about the drinking age...

301. When I get to choose where my family goes on our next vacation...

302. When I'm a parent...

303. When I mow the lawn...

304. When I know I've made my parents happy...

305. When I'm sorry...

306. When I receive a gift...

307. When I think about holding my first child...

308. When someone tells me I'm his or her best friend...

309. When I have surgery...

310. When I hear someone say that he or she is dying...

311. When I do better than I expected to do...

312. When I run out of money and need gas in my car...

313. When I listen to rap music...

314. When I skip school...

315. When I think about cancer...

316. When I'm asked for my advice...

317. When I think about my favorite teacher...

318. When I hear about a new iPod model...

319. When I feel pressured to do something I don't want to do...

320. When I watch the news...

321. When I'm asked if I'm a leader or a follower...

322. When I'm given the choice to watch football or play football...

323. When I think about which spiritual gift(s) I have...

324. When I go to the Christmas Eve service...

325. When I truly feel loved...

326. When I see a stretch limo...

327. When I think about the worst day I ever had...

328. When I go to the mall...

329. When I watch the Olympics...

330. When I see somebody I admire do something terribly wrong...

331. When I go hiking...

332. When I take pictures...

333. When I don't know what to do with my life...

334. When I see a neighborhood full of Christmas lights...

335. When I walk into the youth room at my church...

336. When I go to a wedding...

337. When I think about what it would be like to be the richest person in the world...

338. When I hear there are more than 27 million people living in slavery today...

339. When I think about my past...

340. When I choose where to sit in class...

341. When I hear my alarm go off...

342. When I think about people starving...

343. When I get hyper, I usually...

344. When I go running...

345. When I earn my own money...

346. When I think about what Olympic event I'd like to compete in...

347. When I overeat...

348. When I get the hiccups...

349. When I think about space travel...

350. When I hear someone telling a lie about my friend...

351. When I write...

352. When I think about the thing I haven't done but would most like to do...

353. When I just want to hang out...

354. When I break up with my boyfriend or girlfriend...

355. When I see Mormon missionaries walking down my street...

356. When I feel like my circumstances will never change...

357. When I think about the most creative thing I've ever done...

358. When I go to my next concert, it will be to see...

359. When I think about Jesus dying for my sins...

360. When I'm outside in freezing cold weather...

361. When I hear about steroids being used in professional sports...

362. When I want to have more friends...

363. When I get a chance to use my spiritual gift(s)...

364. When I talk to an atheist...

365. When I go to Disney World...

366. When I hear about same-sex marriage...

367. When I struggle with how to remain pure...

368. When I'm most tempted to swear...

369. When I think about becoming a missionary...

370. When I work out, my favorite way to exercise is...

371. When I spend time on YouTube...

372. When I think about the funniest friend I have...

373. When I hear the word *holy*...

374. When I buy candy at the movie theater...

375. When I play an instrument...

376. When I think about the best gift I've ever received...

377. When I hang out with my cousins...

378. When I go to an animal shelter...

379. When I don't get enough sleep...

380. When I think about my personal relationship with Jesus Christ...

381. When I go to the zoo...

382. When I think about the qualities I most admire in my parents...

383. When I can take a class just for the fun of it, I'll choose...

384. When I visit colleges...

385. When I feel like God doesn't care...

386. When I think about my grades...

387. When I don't like someone, but they like me...

388. When I order eggs in a restaurant, I like them...

389. When I struggle with managing my time...

390. When I see a homeless person asking for money...

391. When I think about a famous person I'd like to meet...

392. When I'm alone...

393. When I get a chance to go on a mission trip...

394. When I think about the skill I'm most proud of...

395. When I see people throw trash on the ground...

396. When I think about the place where I'd most like to go...

397. When I get invited to a party that I know I shouldn't go to...

398. When I'm asked to share my testimony, I usually talk about...

399. When I go swimming...

400. When I hear about Christians being tortured for their faith...

401. When I feel like God doesn't hear my prayers...

402. When I think about the disease I'd most like to see cured...

403. When I'm in an elevator full of people...

404. When I celebrate the Fourth of July, I usually...

405. When I get a chance to talk to Adam and Eve in heaven someday...

406. When I think about being the only Christian in a group of people and being asked about my faith...

407. When I hear about school shootings...

408. When I eat my grandma's cooking...

409. When I have to sit still for more than an hour...

410. When I had my first crush, it was on...

411. When I think back to my favorite Halloween costume...

412. When I'm most impatient is when...

413. When I go skiing, I like to go...

414. When I see TV preachers...

415. When I listen to Christian music...

416. When I read my school newspaper...

417. When I'm the most tempted to overspend is...

418. When I think about the biggest issues facing the church in the next five years...

419. When I'm asked about my favorite brand of clothes...

420. When I've lost hope...

421. When I think about the popular kids at my school...

422. When I don't get to do something I really want to do, but my friend does...

423. When I'm late for curfew...

424. When I hear that a friend's parents are getting a divorce...

425. When I'm riding on a roller coaster...

426. When I'm in a thunderstorm...

427. When I'm failing a class...

428. When I think about the grossest thing I've ever done...

429. When I see the effects of a large hurricane...

430. When I think about eternity...

431. When I need more joy in my life...

432. When I go to my grandparents' house...

433. When I think about the greatest U.S. president...

434. When I have to decide between two good choices...

435. When I see someone crying...

436. When I think back to the first thing that I saved up a lot of money to buy...

437. When I'm on a trampoline...

438. When I'm forced to eat something I don't like...

439. When I think about an event that I'll never forget...

440. When I hear someone use God's name in vain...

441. When I want to treat myself to something special...

442. When I can't sleep...

443. When I pray but my prayers aren't answered the way I want them to be...

444. When I drive through a dangerous neighborhood...

445. When I take (took) the ACT or SAT test...

446. When I see a baby...

447. When I think about how God feels about me...

448. When I'm behind a slow driver and can't get around him or her...

449. When I leave a friend's house...

450. When I'm old and have gray hair...

451. When I don't understand the language being spoken...

452. When I pick up the phone, I'm most likely calling...

453. When I need to borrow money...

454. When I believe my parents like my sibling(s) better than they like me...

455. When I'm given an assignment at the beginning of the quarter that's not due until the end of the quarter...

456. When I celebrate my next birthday, I want to...

457. When I see a snake...

458. When I think about the miracle I'd most like to see Jesus do in my life...

459. When I don't like the song being sung in church...

460. When I think about joining the military...

461. When I get on somebody's nerves, it's usually because...

462. When I'm asked about my religion...

463. When I think about the three people who've had the biggest impact on my life...

464. When I want to encourage someone…

465. When I'm in gym class, the activity I like the most is…

466. When I think about life on other planets…

467. When I have a baby girl, I want to name her…

468. When I have a baby boy, I want to name him...

469. When I struggle with my faith...

470. When I hear a joke I've already heard before...

471. When I'm most at peace...

472. When I think about whose life I'd want if I couldn't have my own...

473. When I perform a random act of kindness...

474. When I hear about someone speaking in tongues...

475. When I struggle most with self-control is...

476. When I hear about demons...

477. When I think about angels...

478. When I get caught in a lie...

479. When I think about God being my Father...

480. When I'm lost...

481. When I think about how my life could be different...

482. When I have regrets...

483. When I'm in a class and I really enjoy the teacher...

484. When I think about God as a judge...

485. When I find out that my family is having company...

486. When I fight with my friends...

487. When I see adults playing video games...

488. When I'm asked which store I'd like a gift card to...

489. When I was a little kid and someone told me a scary story...

490. When I want to tell someone how I feel, but I'm afraid of how that person will react...

491. When I see the price of gasoline...

492. When I struggle with my appearance...

493. When I think about the vastness of the universe...

494. When I don't get invited to a party that I thought I'd be invited to...

495. When I see a house on fire...

496. When I order ice cream...

497. When I think back to my happiest childhood memory...

498. When I play *Guitar Hero*...

499. When I go to the library...

500. When I think about what question should be in the next
When I... book...

Email your ideas to brian_schulenburg@yahoo.com

The best idea I receive each month will be posted on my blog:
http://bschulenburg.blogspot.com

Adapted from Lee Strobel's best-selling books, The Case For... books for students will take them along on his investigations about Christ, faith, and creation. Students will find answers and encouragement that will strengthen their faith.

The Case for the Real Jesus—Student Edition
A Journalist Investigates Current Challenges to Christianity
Lee Strobel with Jane Vogel
RETAIL $9.99
ISBN 978-0-310-28323-2

The Case for Christ—Student Edition
A Journalist's Personal Investigation of the Evidence of Jesus
Lee Strobel with Jane Vogel
RETAIL $9.99
ISBN 978-0-310-23484-5

The Case for a Creator—Student Edition
A Journalist Investigates Scientific Evidence That Points Toward God
Lee Strobel with Jane Vogel
RETAIL $9.99
ISBN 978-0-310-24977-1

The Case for Faith—Student Edition
A Journalist Investigates the Toughest Objections to Christianity
Lee Strobel with Jane Vogel
RETAIL $9.99
ISBN 978-0-310-24188-1

Visit www.planetwisdom.com or your local bookstore.